Mick Manning & Brita Granström
Nature SCHOOL

F

FRANCES LINCOLN
CHILDREN'S BOOKS

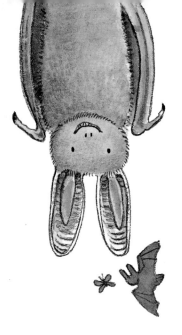

For Eric Sadler and John Norris Wood – my own Nature School teachers – M.M.

Text and illustrations copyright © Mick Manning and Brita Granström 1997
First published in 1997 by Kingfisher, an imprint of Larousse plc

This edition published in Great Britain and in the USA in 2009 by
Frances Lincoln Children's Books, 4 Torriano Mews,
Torriano Avenue, London NW5 2RZ
www.franceslincoln.com

British Library Cataloguing in Publication Data available on request

ISBN 978-1-84507-844-7

Printed in China

9 8 7 6 5 4 3 2 1

Contents

What this book is about!

Hi, I'm Mick ... Welcome to Nature School! Get ready to learn all about the world of nature!

Would you like to recognize different nature sounds and be able to name animal tracks? Would you like to feed hungry birds and keep wild animals safe? **Nature School** teaches you how to do all these things and lots more. **Nature School** is full of exciting projects that will make you feel closer to the world around you.

Useful things

rucksack

plastic bags

packed lunch

garden gloves

washing up gloves

waterproof coat and trousers

NATURE TIPS

Look out for helpful tips in the coloured strips down the side of each page.

*Throughout the book you will see words in **bold type**. You can find out more about these words in the glossary at the back of the book.*

binoculars

a torch

magnifying lens

old clothes

tweezers

a good field guide

old trainers

pencil

notebook

coloured pens

5

toilet paper or cotton wool

tape

whistle

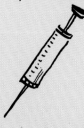
A nature notebook

As you read through **Nature School**, keep a nature notebook – this should be a mixture of a notepad, sketchbook and scrapbook. Write down and draw all the things you see and stick in photos and drawings. Take cuttings from magazines and catalogues and put these in your notebook. Decorate the pages with some of your nature finds such as leaves, seeds, petals and feathers.

When you make drawings of the wildlife you see, write down details of the birds, animals or objects you have seen, such as colours, sounds, shape and size, so that you can look them up in a guide if you need any more information later on.

pine needle

Nature finds

You must never hurt or disturb animals or dig up plants. When we talk about nature finds they must be things you find lying around such as feathers, broken eggshells, bones, shells and pebbles.

23 July

maple leaf ↗

sycamore seeds

a nice leaf

a canada goose →

I wonder what this flower is?

I saw this beetle ↓

some dead flowers I found today

owl feather

butterfly wing eaten by spider!

dandelion seed

lichen

a nice black feather

You have to be very quiet.

Field skills

Wild animals are shy and secretive, so in order to see them you need to learn about field skills.

Sometimes, to reach a good watching place without being seen, you may need to crawl across open ground as quietly as you can.

Try to be 'downwind' of the animal you are watching. This means the wind is coming towards you and the animal will not be able to smell you. If the wind is going towards the animal, it will carry your smell with it.

Most animals rely on their smell and hearing more than their eyesight. So as long as you are downwind of the animal and stay silent, you shouldn't be spotted. Sit quietly with your back against a tree. Don't peep out from behind the tree when watching animals, as any sudden movement may scare them.

8

Make a hide you can wear

PROJECT

You will need ● a net curtain or strawberry net from a garden centre ● green or brown dye ● scissors ● a bucket ● some leaves and grass.

If you use a net curtain you need to dye it first. Mix the dye in a bucket – follow the instructions on the bottle. Soak your net in the dye. Dry the net and put it over your head. Mark where your face is. Cut out a hole for your face. Thread in some leaves and grass. Wear the 'hide' over your head like a poncho.

Wild faces

PROJECT

Human faces often frighten wild animals. Try and disguise yourself using face paints. Make sure you use special non-toxic face paint. Do not use ordinary paint or you will hurt your skin. Try different disguises, such as badger stripes or a brown-faced stoat. Or try green leaf shapes.

NATURE TIPS

If you find a dead bird see if it has a ring on its leg. Rings give information to experts about bird activity. Write down details of where and when you found the ring and post your notes and the ring to the address written on it.

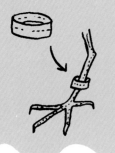

B e a detective and look for the signs that animals leave behind. As well as footprints, tracks and droppings, they leave behind many other clues. You can also look for their homes.

Clues to look for

Gnawed cherry stones and seeds mean voles or mice.

Look out for animal paths under fallen trees or bushes.

Gnawed bark could mean rabbits, squirrels or deer.

Hairs caught on a fence could be from sheep, rabbits or foxes.

Moth and butterfly wings mean a bat, bird or spider has been feeding.

A fish skeleton means an otter or mink has had a tasty meal.

Circles or piles of feathers mean a kill by a predator. If the ends of the feathers are chewed the predator was a mammal. If the feathers are plucked out it was a bird of prey.

Flattened grass where an animal has been lying down.

Is anyone at home?

PROJECT

Put small sticks gently across the entrance of a burrow or animal hole. Any animal entering or leaving the hole will knock the sticks over as it passes. Go back and check the next day. Do not poke the sticks in the hole as this might frighten or hurt the animal if it is at home.

NATURE TIPS

Tiny fishes jumping about could mean a big hungry fish is chasing them.

Circles on the surface of a lake or river could mean that fish are eating insects.

11

Spot some animal homes!

PROJECT

A fox home, like the one in the tree below, is called a den or earth. You can tell if a fox is at home because the entrance will smell musky. If not, then it is empty. Rabbit homes are called warrens. They are burrows in fields, sandy banks and hedges like the three below right. The ground around the entrance is often worn and covered in small round pellets or droppings. You will often find rabbit fur near the holes too.

A 'football' of leaves and twigs tucked in the corner of a branch and trunk is a squirrel's home called a drey. A drilled hole in a tree usually means the nest of a woodpecker. Dry mud around a hole is the work of a nuthatch. Sometimes other birds like starlings steal a woodpecker hole. A bigger hole may be an owl's nest.

Tracks & Droppings

You can learn a lot about animals by studying their tracks and droppings. Look for tracks by muddy paths, puddles, sandy beaches and in snow. If you find a dropping, try and guess whose it is.

Clues to look for

Droppings

Predator (fox)

Vegetarian (deer)

bird or lizard

mouse or vole

Tracks

fox	dog	cat	otter	stoat	mouse	rat	shrew

duck	crow	mini-beast	squirrel	horse	deer	sheep	heron

a hopping rabbit or hare...

a leaping stoat

a fox trotting and leaving a dropping...

Have you had a mystery guest?

PROJECT

Nearly fill a plastic washing-up bowl or other container with soft sand from a garden centre. Smooth over the top.

On a plate put out something for your guests to eat, like dog biscuits, rabbit food or cold porridge – lots of animals love cold porridge! Leave it overnight. Next day, look for tracks. Can you recognize the tracks left in the sand in the drawing?

NATURE TIPS

Don't touch droppings. If you want to examine them poke them with a stick.

Keep a record in your nature notebook of tracks or droppings you find.

Small, white droppings were probably left by a bird or lizard.

Make a cast of tracks!

13

1.

PROJECT

For two small casts you will need:
● a strip of card 40cm long and 6cm wide ● 2 paperclips ● plastic bowl or jug ● a litre bottle of water ● 2 large cupfuls of plaster of Paris ● stick for stirring ● bubble wrap or tissue paper.

1. Find a good, clear track in mud or sand and carefully clear away any twigs or leaves.
2. Bend the strip into a circle to fit around your track and fix it together with the paperclips.
3. Using your stick, mix up the plaster of Paris with enough water to make it into a thick cream.
4. Pour it into your mould. When it is dry, after about twenty minutes, gently lift up the solid plaster of Paris keeping it in the cardboard strip. Carry it home carefully in bubble wrap or tissue paper.

When you get home, clean off the mud or soil with an old toothbrush. Use a marker pen to write on the cast the date and place you found the track and the type of animal you think made it.

2.

3.

4.

Wild life feeding stations

Attract the animals to your garden or windowsill by putting out food. It is best to do this in the winter. Bread isn't really very good for birds – give them leftover foods such as breakfast cereals, bacon rind, cheese, pasta, meaty bones and potatoes. Avoid salty foods and never give them roasted peanuts.

Eating out

PROJECT

Make a simple windowsill feeder by wedging a sturdy stick across a window and hanging various feeders from it. Have a go at making the following recipes. Write down in your nature notebook which birds eat which foods.

Make peanut feeders from big plastic bottles by cutting a hole at the top on one side. Fill with peanuts.

Make bird cake by mixing together peanuts and sunflower seeds with soft lard until it is nice and squidgy. Thread string through the bottom of a plastic yoghurt pot. Fill the pot with the cake mixture.

Chill it in the fridge until the mixture is hard then hang it upside down for bird acrobats.

For a log mobile, ask an adult to drill some holes of different sizes into two dead branches. Stuff the holes with lard or fat. Tie the branches together in a criss-cross shape. Hang it outside at least two metres high.

Bird apple pie

PROJECT

Take an old plastic bowl outside. Using your foot, squash up some old bruised apples. Spoon the apples into the bowl. Cover with a layer of porridge oats, peanuts and sunflower seeds. Put the bowl on your bird table and watch who comes to eat from it.

Potato surprise

PROJECT

Some birds are too shy to get to a window feeder or bird table so here is a recipe especially for them. Stuff a baked potato with nuts, cheese and seeds. Leave it in a quiet corner away from prowling cats. Write down who comes to eat it.

Make a feeding station

PROJECT

It is easy to make a feeding station – ask a grown up to nail an old tray to a wooden post like this. Make sure the table is high enough to be out of the reach of cats. Keep it clean of old bits of food.

Cut up bacon rind into small pieces for robins.

Put sunflower seeds in one of the feeders on your windowsill to attract finches.

Bluetits love pecking at peanuts in a netbag – make sure the nuts are not salted or roasted.

15

Badgers love dog biscuits, cold porridge and raisins. If they do visit your garden, watch from a window so that you don't frighten them.

Animal homes

Once you have attracted animals to feed in your garden or yard why not make them some homes to live in – then you can study them even more. Animal homes can be hand-made by you, bought from a shop or just places you leave to become wild and overgrown.

Minibeast motel

PROJECT

Not all animals are cute and cuddly, but they are still interesting to watch. A melon makes a good motel for snails, slugs, woodlice, bugs and beetles. Halve a melon or grapefruit and eat the inside. Cut a door in one side with your spoon. Put the melon upside-down in a damp corner out of the sun. Peep inside every morning to see how many guests are staying. The motel won't last long because the bugs will eat it bit by bit.

MOTEL

Build a wild shelter
PROJECT

A pile of old branches, dead leaves and hedge clippings with grass and nettles growing, makes a good home for lizards, wild mice, hedgehogs and small birds. If you don't have a garden put down some soil in a grow bag, then scatter nettle and thistle seeds on top. Next lay branches on top in a criss-cross pattern. Make sure there are lots of gaps to let in light and to give your visitors room to move around. To study the animals, sit by the pile very quietly and watch who comes and goes.

NATURE TIPS

Always remember to keep your animal homes away from cats and dogs and other dangers.

Hang a net bag of peanuts (not salted) or fat on your box throughout the winter so the birds know that the box is there.

Fix your bird box in a shady spot facing north to south east.

17

Bird box
PROJECT

Ask a grown up to make a bird box for you – it's easy! Make one from marine plywood or timber by following the plan on this page. Once you have cut out your pieces hold them together with strong nails. Or you can buy a bird box from the **RSPB** or from a garden centre or pet shop.

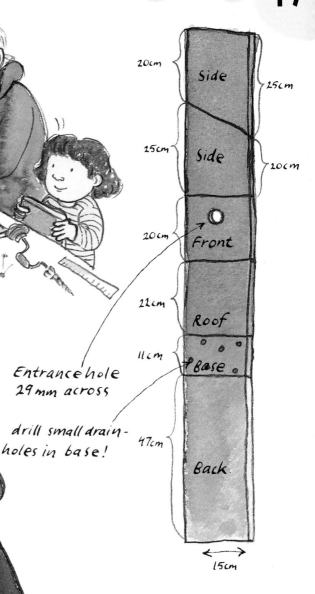

20cm — Side — 25cm

15cm — Side — 10cm

20cm — Front

Entrance hole 29mm across

22cm — Roof

11cm — Base

drill small drain-holes in base!

47cm — Back

15cm

Minibeasts

Minibeasts can be found everywhere – thousands can live in just a handful of dead leaves. Minibeasts are small invertebrates (animals without a backbone) and include insects, spiders and worms. Some are vegetarians and feed on leaves and some are predators and eat the vegetarians. When you try the following projects, make notes and drawings in your nature notebook about what different minibeasts look like.

You will need ● a paper funnel ● a sweet jar ● black paper ● a table lamp ● sticky tape ● some damp tissue ● magnifying glass.

Minibeast funnel

PROJECT

Wrap the black paper around the jar and tape in place. Put a sheet of damp tissue in the bottom of the jar. Put the funnel in the jar. Wearing gloves, take a handful of dead leaves and put them in the funnel. Shine your light on top of the leaves (not too close) and leave it for an hour. When you come back, some of the tiny minibeasts will have dropped into the jar. Look closely at them, using a magnifying glass. Draw how they look in your nature notebook.

We are all minibeasts!

Check a plant

PROJECT

One healthy plant can be home to lots of different kinds of minibeasts. Find a plant like a nettle or rosebush and see how many minibeasts you can see living on it. Be careful not to scratch or sting yourself. What minibeasts can you see living on this plant?

NATURE TIPS

A magnifying glass is useful for looking at minibeasts.

Always wear gloves when picking up leaves or studying plants.

Check out a rotten log

harvestman

wood beetle

millipede

beetle grub

centipede

weevil

woodlouse

rove beetle

PROJECT

Find a rotten log and check out how many minibeasts are living on it, in it and under it. What can you find? Worms, beetles and centipedes, perhaps? Draw them in your nature notebook. Think about the sort of minibeasts that might live among rotten logs and leaves and write a list of them in your nature notebook.

19

Fungi

The first thing to learn about fungi (also called mushrooms or toadstools) is that some are very poisonous and you should never eat them or put your fingers in your mouth after touching them. But you can have fun collecting the different sorts and drawing the patterns on the underside of their caps.

Spore prints

PROJECT

Fungi scatter a dust-like powder, called spores, which grow into new fungi. Lay some edible mushroom caps on squares of paper and leave them overnight. Next day, carefully lift them up and you will see that they have left patterns of spores on the paper. To stop the spore dust flying off the paper or smudging, spray them very gently with hairspray. Do not hold the hairspray too close to the paper. Stick the patterns in your nature notebook or on your bedroom wall.

Spot different shapes

Next time you go on a nature walk, see how many different fungi shapes you can find.

Growing Mould

PROJECT

Mould is a small sort of fungus that grows from tiny spores that float in the air all around us. Take an old bruised apple or a piece of bread and put it in a jar. Put the lid on with some air holes. Soon the mould will begin to grow. Watch your mould grow and develop until it covers all of the fruit. Once this has happened, throw away the jar.

NATURE TIPS

Wear gloves when touching fungi and wash your hands afterwards.

Grow mould from different bits of food, such as cheese, fruit and bread, and see how different each mould looks.

When you have grown your mould in the jar, paint it in your nature notebook. Use coloured pencils or watercolours.

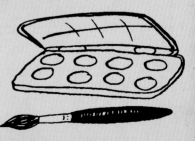

Worm farm

Worms are very helpful. They eat dead leaves and aerate the soil with their tunnels. They help fertilise the soil, too. Worms are both male and female in one body. Animals like this are called hermaphrodites.

Make a worm farm

PROJECT

You will need ● a plastic bottle ● a large jar ● soil and sand ● elastic band ● black paper ● sticky tape ● leaves and grass ● tights or other mesh material for the lid. Cut the bottom off the plastic bottle and put the bottle in the large jar. Pour layers of soil and sand in the space between the bottle and the jar and make it damp. Collect some worms and put them on top of the soil and sand. Put some leaves and grass on top for them to eat. Stretch the mesh material over the top of the jar to make a lid. Wrap the black paper around the jar and fix it in position with tape. Leave the jar in a cool place for a couple of days. When you take off the paper, you will see the worms' tunnels. You must let the worms go after a week or they may die.

22

cut a plastic bottle

sand and soil

leaves for food

black paper

mesh for lid

elastic band

Dances with worms!

Birds call worms to the surface by stamping on the ground. See if you can do this by trying this special worm dance. Gently stamp your feet and move around on a patch of earth or grass. After about five minutes stop and see if any worms have come to the surface. Write how many have appeared in your nature notebook.

23

Listen to the worms

PROJECT

Put a worm or two on a sheet of paper. Put your ear close to the paper and listen. Can you hear the worms' bristles scratching as they crawl along? The bristles help the worms to get a grip. Remember to put the worms back where you found them.

Changing bodies

Metamorphosis is the name for the way some animals change their shape completely as they grow, like a caterpillar turning into a butterfly or a grub into a ladybird. Butterflies have very delicate wings with tiny scales on like dust so try not to touch them with your fingers.

caterpillars

Butterflies are insects that fly by day and have brightly coloured wings. Butterflies like to feed on flowers and sunbathe in warm places. A butterfly starts life as an egg which hatches into a caterpillar. The caterpillar feeds on plants and later turns into a chrysalis. The butterfly forms inside the chrysalis.

egg

caterpillar

chrysalis

butterfly leaving chrysalis

24

PROJECT

Look around wild plants and cabbage patches to find some common caterpillars. Put them in a box or jar with leaves from the plant you found them on. Put a net lid on the jar, such as fine mesh tights, so that they get plenty of light and fresh air – use sticky tape or an elastic band to hold the lid in place. Every day, take out the old leaves and put in fresh leaves for them to eat and twigs to crawl on. As the caterpillars grow and change draw the different stages of the metamorphosis in your nature notebook. When the caterpillars turn into chrysalises be patient and do not touch them. When the butterflies hatch let them dry their wings and then, very gently, let them go.

NATURE TIPS

Make a tall home for your caterpillars by cutting the top off one plastic bottle and the top and bottom off another. Join the two plastic bottles together with sticky tape. Cover the top with fine mesh and hold in place with tape.

Grow plants for butterflies

PROJECT

To attract butterflies, plant buddleia and Michaelmas daisies in your garden and catmint, aubrietia and marjoram in a window box.

25

Look at ladybirds

Ladybirds also go through several different stages. The adult ladybird lays eggs which turn into grubs, then pupae, then more adults.

ladybird

eggs

pupa

grub

You can keep ladybirds too! But they are predators and have to have a fresh supply of leaves with aphids and plant bugs on every day to eat.

Nuts, beans, cones and seeds

Nuts and seeds grow into new plants and trees. Beans and seeds come in all shapes and sizes. You can get them from shops or look for them on your nature walks.

Runner beans

PROJECT

Line a glass jar with damp blotting paper and fill with soil, newspaper or cotton wool to hold the blotting paper tight against the jar. Push some runner beans, broad beans or sunflower seeds between the jar and the blotting paper. Put the jar in a warm, dark place until the beans and seeds begin to sprout. Check the jar every day. Draw the changes in your nature notebook.

Farm your own crop

PROJECT

This is a sort of farming – growing plants for food. You will need ● a saucer ● cotton wool or blotting paper ● mung beans from a health food shop.

1.

2.

3.

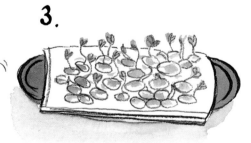

4.

1. Put some wet cotton wool or blotting paper on a saucer or in a jar. **2.** Put the saucer in a warm place and make sure you keep the cotton wool or blotting paper wet by spraying it with water. **3.** Soon the beans will sprout and begin to grow. **4.** After two or three days the beans should be big enough for you to cut and add to a salad. So now you can say you are a farmer! Try growing other beans for sandwiches and salads.

Plant a nut

PROJECT

Next time you go on a nature walk collect some acorns, chestnuts and other nuts. Soak some of them in a bowl overnight. The next day, plant each nut in a separate pot. Label it with a lollipop stick. Leave some indoors and put some outdoors over the winter. If you are lucky, by the spring tiny oak or chestnut trees may have begun to grow. In your nature notebook write down which nuts grew first, the indoor or the outdoor ones? Keep a record of how quickly they grow.

NATURE TIPS

Collect some pine cones. Put some in a warm, dry place and some in a damp place. If there is moisture in the air the cone will stay tightly shut. In the warmth, the cone will open ready to spread its seeds. If you leave a pine cone on a window-sill or outside the back or front door, you will be able to tell what the weather is going to be like.

27

Cone prints

On your next nature walk, collect some cones. Cones carry the seeds of conifer trees. Cones have woody scales to protect their small seeds from damage. In warm weather they open up and the seeds flutter away on the breeze hopefully to grow into new conifers. Most cones stay on the tree for a year before their seeds are ready. To make cone prints, roll out some coloured modelling clay and press different sorts of cones into it. Keep a note of the patterns and which tree each cone came from.

How Seeds spread

Seeds spread in lots of different ways - some stick to fur and jumpers, some float in the air, some fly like helicopter blades, some are spread in animal droppings. How many can you find and record in your nature notebook? Berries are cases for seeds – they are soft fruits with lots of little seeds inside. Some berries are very poisonous, so don't eat or touch any wild berries that you find.

Berries for birds

The seeds of berries, such as raspberries and blackberries, are spread by birds and animals who eat the soft fruit. The seeds are then spread in their droppings. Collect some berries, put them out for the birds and note down who eats what.

Plants from your shoes

You can spread seeds as well! To prove it, grow some plants from your shoes. After a nature walk, scrape the mud from your shoes into a plant pot. Water it. Put it outdoors and watch it grow. Do you recognize any of the plants?

Make a fruit Salad

PROJECT

Most fruits have seeds inside. Some of them you can eat, some you can't. Buy some of your favourite fruits. Cut them in half. Quickly sketch the patterns the seeds or pips make. Later on, you can draw these in your nature notebook and colour them in. Slice the fruit. Put to one side the pips or seeds you can't eat for the next project. Put the fruit pieces into a bowl. Pour over some fruit juice and a little sugar to taste. Mix the fruit salad together and serve with cream, ice cream or on its own.

You can make a sycamore nose like this...

Plant the Seeds

PROJECT

Plant some of the fruit pips in yoghurt pots or plant pots. Make small holes in the bottom of the pots for drainage. Fix a plastic bag over the top of the pot using an elastic band. Bend a straw into the bag. Blow into it to make the bag blow up. You now have a mini greenhouse for your fruit to grow in. Label the pots. Remember to take the bag off once the seeds start sprouting.

Trees

Trees can grow to be the biggest things on Earth! A tree is a plant and like all plants it uses sunlight to make food and grow. Trees help us by making oxygen for us to breathe and by absorbing poisonous gases like carbon dioxide. Trees can live for many hundreds of years. To find out how old a tree is measure around the trunk. Every 2.5 centimetres stands for about a year in the tree's life.

Hugging a tree

PROJECT

Hug a tree! Close your eyes and feel the texture of the bark. Smell the trunk. Listen to the sounds around the tree like insects buzzing and birds singing. Hug five different trees and write down the textures, smells and noises of each in your nature notebook. Collect some leaves that have fallen off the tree. Make a bark rubbing. Put all these things together in your notebook to get an overall picture of each tree.

Bark rubbings

PROJECT

Make a set of bark rubbings to go with your pressed leaves and nature notes. Use sheets of cartridge paper and a big wax crayon to get the best results. Rub gently and don't damage the tree trunk. When you get home try washing over the rubbing with a watery paint – this will make it even clearer. Remember to label the tree it came from and where you did the bark rubbing.

Red celery

PROJECT

Mix some red ink with water in a jar or vase. Put in a stick of celery and watch what happens over the next day or two. The leaves should turn pink – this shows how water is carried around a tree. A tree can have as much as 100 litres of water moving around inside it.

Pressed leaves

PROJECT

To press leaves for your nature notebook, place the leaves between sheets of blotting paper. Press them between two heavy books – you could add a brick for extra weight!

NATURE TIPS

Night-time animals are called nocturnal.

Moths are night-flying insects that look like butterflies, but tend to have duller coloured wings. If you keep any moths to study, always let them go at night, not during the day.

32

Night-time and moths

As the sun goes down, listen carefully to what you can hear. Frogs may be calling, crickets may be chirping, birds may be singing. We call this time of day dusk.

PROJECT

Listen to the night noises. Write down who you think is making each noise. Make sound patterns on a sheet of paper. Use a different colour for each sound. When you have finished, you will have composed a sheet of night music. Listen for the birds singing early in the morning, too. That's called the dawn chorus. Compose a sheet of dawn chorus music too!

Sugaring

PROJECT

Mix together some concentrated blackcurrant squash with a pint of hot water then dissolve two tablespoons of syrup or treacle and four tablespoons of sugar in it. Paint the mixture on a fence or tree trunk. Best of all, soak a bunch of rags and hang them up. In the evening keep a check on it to see if moths come and feed.

Hang up a sheet

PROJECT

Another good way to spot moths and other night-time insects is to hang up a white sheet on a washing line or tree. When it gets dark, shine a spotlight or electric flashlight on to it. Soon, moths will come and land on the sheet. Have a good look at them. See if they are different from ones you've seen before.

Moths are night-flying insects...

Bats and owls

Bats are brilliant night-time hunters. They eat hundreds of insects every night. They live in old buildings, caves, hollow trees and roof spaces. Owls are beautiful, mysterious birds. Most owls are nocturnal (active at night) but some can be diurnal (active during the day).

Bat ears

PROJECT

Bats are not blind but they hunt in the dark using echolocation – this means that they listen to the echo of their own squeaks bouncing off objects in the dark. This is how they can 'see' well enough in the dark to catch insects and not to crash into things. Make two paper funnels like the one in the drawing. Hold one to each ear – you will soon understand why a bat's ears are so big.

34

How to make an owl hoot

Clasp your hands together like this.

Bend your thumbs slightly to make a hole. Blow into the hole.

PROJECT

Talk to owls by making hooting noises with your hands. Hoot out of your window at night – you never know, occasionally an owl may hoot back!

Hide and squeak!

PROJECT

Copy the mouse and owl drawings shown above on to a sheet of thin card and colour them in. Make a hole either side of each mask. Thread a length of elastic, long enough to fit round your head, through the holes and knot the ends. Cut eye holes so that you can see clearly. You only need one owl mask but make plenty of mice masks. Try adding fishing line 'whiskers' on the mice! Then invite your friends round to play 'hide and squeak'! One of you has to be the owl. The others are mice. The mice go and hide and make squeaking noises while the owl tries to find them. The last mouse he finds becomes the owl for the next game.

Owl pellets

Owls are birds of prey. They feed on small mammals and birds and then they make pellets. Pellets are small balls of fur and bones coughed up after a meal. You can find pellets wherever owls sleep, perch and nest.

Here are things you might find...

PROJECT

Look for owl pellets under trees, fences and poles. Put a pellet in an old tin can or mug and pour some warm water over it and a little disinfectant. Let it soak for ten minutes. Tip out the water and put the pellet on a sheet of paper. Gently pull it apart with two old forks or a pair of tweezers.

Litter and Pollution

Litter can hurt wild animals – even rubbish thrown away in a bag can be dangerous to wildlife if the bag is torn open. To be absolutely safe, and to help the environment generally, recycle as much rubbish as you can. Take old bottles and newspapers to special recycling bins – if you don't know where your nearest bins are ask your local council. If you have a garden, start a compost heap with waste scraps of food such as vegetable peelings, eggshells and used teabags.

Bottles

Thrown away bottles become death traps for insects and other small animals. They crawl inside and slip down the neck of the bottle. Once inside they are trapped. If you find a thrown away bottle, block up the neck with paper and insert a stick – this will stop animals crawling in, and help minibeasts to crawl out! If you can, put the bottle in a bag and throw it in a bin. Never pick up broken bottles.

Tin Cans

Scavenging animals and birds can get tin cans stuck on their nose or beak when they poke around dustbins and rubbish tips. To stop this happening, squash all cans before you throw them away. Carefully tuck the lid into the can and squash it by stamping on it. What would you do if you were a fox with a tin can stuck on your nose? Write a story about how you would get it off in your notebook.

Other dangers...

Plastic rings that hold together cans of beer can get stuck around the necks of animals. Always cut the rings with scissors before you throw them away. Nylon string or old fishing line can get tangled around the legs or necks of animals and birds. Cut them into short lengths before throwing away and never leave fishing line lying around. Always put litter in a bin.

Oil pollution

Sometimes, large amounts of oil are poured into the seas by ships which have crashed or because there has been an accident on an oil rig. When this happens seals and sea birds get oil clogged in their fur or feathers and they drown or swallow poisonous oil. Imagine that you are a bird that has swum into a patch of oil. What does it feel like? What would you do next? Write the story in your nature notebook.

NATURE TIPS

If you find an injured creature, gently cover it with a coat or towel before picking it up. Keep it away from your face (be particularly careful of sharp beaks). Keep quiet around them and don't make sudden movements. Always phone a wildlife rescue service (keep the number in your notebook). A cardboard box is a safe, dark place to keep a creature until help arrives.

Acid rain

A serious sort of **pollution** is caused by chemicals from factories and chimneys which go into the sky as dirty smoke and fall back to Earth as acid rain.

PROJECT

Put some vinegar in a glass or jar and drop in a piece of white chalk. Watch what happens. This is how acid rain dissolves stonework in buildings, although it happens much more slowly than your experiment.

37

PROJECT

Pick some leaves with their stalks. Stand them in a cup or jar of vinegar for a few days. Write down what happens in your nature notebook. This is a speeded up version of what acid rain does to trees.

Keep a list of any pollution you find near your home, whatever it is. Can you see any signs of acid rain pollution like brown patches on leaves or dead branches or partly dissolved statues or stones?

Make a pond

NATURE TIPS

Remember to keep your pond topped up in hot weather so that animals are able to crawl in and out easily. Put in a log bridge to help them.

If you have younger brothers or sisters, ask a grown up to cover your pond with chicken wire or a fence to keep them from falling in.

Ponds are important for all sorts of wildlife both as homes and as places to come and drink. You don't need a big garden to have a pond – you can even make a pond in a jam jar!

Pond in a bowl

Make your very own pond. You can make it in an old plastic washing-up bowl, a bucket or even an old sink.

1.

2.

You will need ● a washing-up bowl ● big and small stones ● pondweed from a garden centre ● some soil or sand.
1. Take the plastic bowl and dig it into the soil or place it in a quiet corner in your garden or yard. Cover the bottom with sand. Put in some small stones and also a couple of bigger stones that will poke above the surface of the water.
2. Put in some pondweed to keep the water fresh and healthy. Tie clumps of the pondweed to the stones to keep it on the bottom.

3. Once you have prepared it, carefully fill your pond to the brim with clear water. Pile stones and old logs around the edge as a shelter for bugs and **amphibians**. After a few weeks all sorts of tiny creatures and plants will begin to live there. Birds will drink and bathe in it, and perhaps frogs, newts and colourful dragonflies will come to visit or stay. Keep notes and drawings in your notebook of the interesting things that happen in your pond in a bowl. Don't take any frogs or newts from the wild because they may already have somewhere to live. But they might come to you. Remember to make them a little ramp to help them climb in and out of the pond.

Pond in a jar!

PROJECT

If you don't have space for a pond in a bowl, you can make a smaller pond in a jar. Fill a clean jar with tiny stones, weed and water, and leave it on your window sill for a few weeks. All sorts of tiny creatures like water fleas and **algae** will come and live there. If you fill your jar with water from an existing pond the number of creatures in your jar will be even higher.

Water World

If you visit the seaside, see if you can find a rock pool. The creatures who live in rock pools have their homes topped up twice a day when the tide comes in.

Make an under water viewer

PROJECT

Reflections on the surface of the water can make it difficult to see into the pool. You can make an underwater viewer to see better. You will need ● a plastic bottle ● plastic bag or clingfilm ● waterproof tape ● scissors ● a pen. Cut off the bottom of the bottle. Stretch the plastic bag or clingfilm across the bottom of the bottle and tape to keep in place. Push below the surface of the rock pool and peep through the top. Sit quietly and see what animals you can spot. Look for small fishes and shrimps hiding in the seaweed. Never take plants or creatures out of the rock pool. Do know the names of the creatures in this rock pool?

See inside a shell

The empty shells you find at the seaside are the old homes of shellfish. These can be wonderful shapes. Look closely and you will see rings, a bit like the lines on a tree trunk, made as the shellfish grew.

Hold a shell to your ear – can you hear the sea? Rub an empty shell against a sheet of sandpaper. Slowly you will rub away one side of the shell and be able to see inside. Draw the different shapes you find.

NATURE TIPS

Never go near deep pools or get cut off by the tide. Stay away from slippery rocks and deep water. Always tell a grown up where you are going.

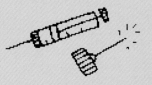

Don't touch anything that looks sharp or dangerous. Even small sea creatures can hurt you. Wear a pair of old trainers.

Don't poke or collect live sea creatures.

41

What can you find on the beach?

shells

feather

bird skull

crab claw

razor shell

egg case

seaweed holding a pebble

shell

shell

crab

pebble

seaweeds

Nature displays

All through this book you have been collecting your nature finds. To show them to your family and friends, why not put them on display? Here are some suggestions...

Feathers

You can find dropped feathers almost anywhere. Small ones come from the body and large ones come from the wings. Display them by sticking them into pieces of polystyrene or modelling clay. Label them with the name of the bird you think they have come from.

Fossils

Fossils are the remains of animals that lived millions of years ago which have become pressed together with sand or mud to become stone. You can find stones with fossils in them by the seaside, riverbank or even in your backyard. Look for patterns in pebbles like the one drawn here. Smooth pebbles or shiny crystals would look nice in your collection, too.

Storage

If you don't want to put your finds on display straight away, make sure you store them carefully once you have cleaned and labelled them. Pack them in biscuit tins filled with newspaper or cotton wool. For small things, use empty matchboxes or chocolate boxes.

Make a display box

PROJECT

Cardboard boxes are good for showing off your finds. Ask at supermarkets and fruit shops for empty boxes. Make a display case like this: measure the inside edges of a cardboard box. Cut cardboard strips to fit. Make slits to fit the strips together. Slot them together to make shelves and put them in your box. Tiny display boxes can be made from the inside of a large matchbox with clingfilm stretched across the front and taped to the back of the box.

Clean up a skull

If you find an animal or bird skull scrub it clean with an old toothbrush in disinfected water. Then leave it outside so that the sun can bleach it white naturally. Always wear rubber gloves when cleaning found things and wash your hands and scrub under your nails afterwards so that you don't catch any germs.

Find out more

Find out more about nature. Visit your local library and look up the birds, animals, minibeasts or objects you have found. Make notes about them for your nature notebook. Find out if there is a young naturalists society in your area or a birdwatching group you can join. Some areas now have special activities and nature trails in local parks and wooded areas. You can also read about the birds and other creatures that live in different parts of the world.

Nature walk

Do you enjoy listening to birds singing in spring, or hearing the wind blowing through the trees in autumn? Would you like to see animals in the wild? If the answers are yes, then you have started to develop your feelings for nature. So put on some comfortable shoes, grab your notebook, and let's go for a walk. Nature walks are also an ideal opportunity to find things for your nature displays.

Listen to nature

Choose a quiet place, it could be in your backyard or garden, in a park or in the countryside, depending on where you live. Sit quietly and write down all the sounds you can hear. Try to describe each sound in words like trickling water, rustling leaves, buzzing insects or squeaking animals.

Smell nature

Choose three different natural things, like a flower, a stone and a leafy branch. Take a good sniff at each one! Try to write down a description of the smells in your nature notebook.

45

Look closer!

Choose somewhere that you can get to easily and safely and that you like very much. Now get down on all fours and have a really close look at the hidden details of nature on the ground. Amazing, isn't it!

NATURE TIPS

Have a nature quiz. Write out ten questions like, 'Guess how many acorns there are in this jar?' or, 'Whose feather is this?' Give the correct answers at the end of the quiz and a nature prize for the winner.

Nature Party

At the end of your nature school have a nature party! Invite your friends and parents to see your nature notebook and your collections and displays. Ask everyone to come dressed as their favourite animal, insect or plant. Play some nature music and make some nature party food – salad with beansprouts, fruit, bread and honey.

Have fun!

Glossary

Aerate
Worm tunnels let air into the soil and this helps to make soil very healthy.

Algae
Tiny plants that grow in fresh or saltwater or on moist ground.

Amphibians
Cold-blooded creatures with a backbone which live on land but breed in water. Frogs, toads and newts are all amphibians.

Caps
The tops of mushrooms and fungi.

Carbon dioxide
A gas in the air that can be poisonous to animals if there is too much of it.

Compost heap
A way of recycling kitchen and garden waste and using it to make fertiliser for your garden – it makes a good home for animals too.

Conifer
Trees or shrubs that bear cones and have evergreen leaves shaped like needles.

Environment
A word used to describe the world we live in.

Oxygen
An invisible gas in the air that all animals need to breathe to stay alive.

Pollution
A word used to describe threats to our environment made by human waste products and litter.

Predator
An animal that eats other animals.

Recycle
This means using things like glass, paper, plastic and aluminium more than once.

Recycling bins
Places you can take glass, cans and paper so that they can be made into new things.

RSPB
These letters stand for the Royal Society for the Protection of Birds. You can write to them for information at: The Lodge, Sandy, Bedfordshire SG19 2DL.

Vegetarian
An animal that just eats plants.

Nature
SCHOOL
Certificate

I have completed

Nature
SCHOOL

with excellence

Mick Manning – Tutor

Mick Manning.